TO
NO MORE

PART SEVEN

By Steve Bush

INTRODUCTION

Nearly five years have elapsed since the first volume of this series was published. Back then the book was conceived as a rather quirky collection of photographs depicting ships in their final days.

That initial volume heralded a flood of material into the Maritime Books office and widespread demand for another volume. To this day that demand continues to grow. However, even more surprising, is that readers are continuing to produce fascinating pictures of all manner of ship from around the country. Pictures that record the end of the battleship era as these leviathans were quickly reduced to scrap metal; post war destroyers laid up by the dozen awaiting a call for return to service that seldom came; modern-day warships, no longer required since the demise of the Cold War, hoping to find a new buyer, but, more often than not, being towed to the shipbreakers.

But what is it about the subject that encourages people to travel to often remote sites to record these images? What is the fascination with these rusting warships? Why are there not volumes of books depicting car breakers, or recording the dismantling of fighter aircraft? The reason, I think, is that every ship, no matter how large the class, is a one off, an individual. Vessels which carry their own names and, throughout sometimes long and illustrious lives, adopt a character and reputation of their own which remains with them throughout their active life with the fleet.

The same cannot be said of other machinery of war. When old, bold fighter pilots sit and reminisce over a picture of a Spitfire they are looking at one of over 22,000 such aircraft. But as old sailors look at a picture of a ship they are looking not at a piece of war machinery, but at a home. A place where they lived, worked, fought, ate and slept for months on end. A ship with it's own individual story to tell.

Unlike aircraft, cars, tanks, the romantic idea of preservation is, in many cases, unrealistic. Costs involved are enormous, maintenance continuous and suitable locations few and far between. For most warships, scrapping is the ultimate fate. This book therefore "rounds the circle", marking the final chapter in the life of many of the Royal Navy's finest warships.

There is something rather sad about seeing a discarded ship laying at her moorings awaiting her fate. Perhaps there is an argument for extending the useful life of todays expensive warships; for re-instating a Reserve Fleet. Over the past few years many relatively young and costly ships have been discarded as an economy measure. In these uncertain times a wise person would be planning for every contingency. Laying ships up in Extended Readiness, maintained by a civilian contractor would release personnel for the frontline fleet, but also maintain a core reserve at little cost. Maybe the next edition will carry pictures of a new generation of reserve ships on Fountain Lake!

A series such as this relies heavily on contributions from private individuals. This volume would not have been possible without their valuable contributions. I would however, like to acknowledge three people in particular. Firstly Norman MacFarlane, Sales Manager at Shipbreaking Industries, who seemed to have his camera with him every day to record the end of so many vessels at Faslane during the height of the shipbreaking industry. Michael Lennon for his superb portraits of the Reserve Ships on Fareham Creek and the comings and goings at Portsmouth. Finally, thanks go to David Hill, for his extensively captioned photographs of submarines at Pound's Yard, Portsmouth.

Steve Bush
April 2002

First published in the United Kingdom in 2002 by Maritime Books, Lodge Hill, Liskeard, Cornwall, PL14 4EL

Some ships careers are brought to a rather premature end. HMS RALEIGH was barely a year old when she was wrecked in thick fog on 8 August 1922. She ran aground on Point Amour on the Labrador side of the Strait of Belle Isle whilst serving with the 8th Light Cruiser Squadron on the Americas and West indies station. Such was the damage that she was declared a total loss and scrapped.
(Syd Goodman Collection)

The Battleship COLOSSUS is seen here on 5 September 1928 arriving at Rosyth in tow of the tugs KINGS CROSS and SAMPHIRE BATTS. A veteran of the Battle of Jutland (the only British Battleship to be hit by gunfire during the engagement) she was sold at Devonport on 25 August 1928 for £71,500 to Charleston Shipbreaking Industries and later resold to Metal Industries.
(Dunfermline Central Library)

Another Jutland veteran - the Iron Duke class battleship MARLBOROUGH is seen arriving at Rosyth in June 1932 after a six day tow from Portsmouth. For the final years of her life the ship was assigned to the Experimental Service where she was used for internal explosion experiments from July to August 1931. These were followed in the spring of 1932 by aerial bombing tests.

(Dunfermline Central Library)

Not all redundant ships made it safely to the shipbreakers. The Admiralty "R" class destroyer TORRID was one of fifteen laid up destroyers that were to be transferred to Wards in part exchange for the liner MAJESTIC, which the Admiralty wished to convert into the TS CALEDONIA. TORRID was handed over to Wards on 27 January 1937. Unfortunately, on 16 March that year, she was wrecked near Trefusis Point, Cornwall, while being towed to Hayle. She was broken up in situ in 1940. (Syd Goodman Collection)

By the time this picture was taken on 27 September 1949, very little remained of the aircraft carrier FURIOUS. Evolving into a carrier through several lengthy reconstructions she served as one of the most successful of the fully converted carriers throughout World War II. She was paid off into reserve in 1944 and sold to T.W. Wards on 15 March 1948 for breaking up at Dalmuir. Just over a year later all that remained was the lower hull on the beaching ground at Troon. Clearly visible are the openings for the four shaft arrangement capable of translating the 90,000 shp into speeds of up to 31.5 knots. (T.W. Ferrers-Walker)

The once graceful bow is the only remaining identifying feature of RENOWN, the only Royal Navy battlecruiser to survive World War II. Having arrived at Metal Industries yard at Faslane on 8 August 1948 she had almost been stripped to the waterline when this picture was taken on 27 September the following year.
(T.W. Ferrers-Walker)

Another anonymous piece of metal lying on the beaching ground at Troon 14 November 1949. It was all that remained of RAMILLIES. She had the distinction of starting her life with two groundings. When launched on 12 September 1916 her bottom hit the underside of the slipway resulting in serious damage to her keel plating and rudders. Whilst being manoeuvred down river on 7 May 1917 following temporary repairs, she again grounded and was not freed until 23 May! (T.W. Ferrers-Walker)

The cruiser JAMAICA shortly after arriving in Gareloch to be laid up. She had paid off into reserve on 5 September 1958 and was moved to the Gareloch for lay up. The only concession to preservation would appear to be a couple of funnel covers and some covers over the close range armament. She was handed over to BISCO on 14 November 1960 and arrived at Arnott Young at Dalmuir to be broken up. Demolition was completed at Troon by 15 August 1963. (I. Muir)

Both ESKIMO and JAVELIN followed similar post war careers. After spending time in reserve at Harwich both ships were allocated to the Ships Trials Committee on 21 February 1948. They later undertook various shock trials in the Gareloch and Loch Striven. Both ships are seen here at Troon on 10 November 1949, JAVELIN (left) shortly after arrival and ESKIMO almost six months into the demolition process. (T.W. Ferrers-Walker)

After a short post war career on the East Indies Station the cruiser NORFOLK arrived at Devonport on 3 May 1949 to reduce to reserve. She was moved to the River Fal on 3 November that year for lay-up before departing (under tow of ENGLISHMAN) on 19 February 1950 bound for Cashmore's shipbreakers at Newport. She is seen here shortly after arrival - on 14 March 1950. (T.W. Ferrers-Walker)

What a difference a few short months can make. The same ship on 2 August, only 5 months later, with just the double bottom sitting on the mud. (T.W. Ferrers-Walker)

It's September 1953 and the incomplete HERCULES had already been laid up in the Gareloch for six years. In January 1957, however, she was sold to India and in April the same year arrived at Harland and Wolff Shipbuilders in Belfast for reconstruction and modernisation. She emerged in 1961 and on 4 March that year was commissioned into the Royal Indian Navy as VIKRANT. She survives to this day (2002) as a museum ship at Mumbai (Bombay) after nearly forty years active service. (I. Muir)

Completed in December 1943 FLINT CASTLE was assigned to the Clyde Escort Force until the end of the war. There followed a 10 year period with the 2nd Training Squadron at Portland before finally being placed in reserve at Devonport in 1956. She arrived at Faslane on 10 July 1958 for scrapping.

(T.W. Ferrers-Walker)

At the time, the newest of the Royal Navy's conventional cruisers - SUPERB - was laid up on the Gareloch in 1957, lack of funds preventing a modernisation refit. Pictured here on 17 September 1958 she was moved the short distance to Dalmuir in August 1960 for scrapping, being moved again to Troon on 16 May 1961 for final demolition. (I. Muir)

The DUKE OF YORK arrived at Faslane for breaking up on 18 February 1958 direct from lay up on the Gareloch. This view taken on 26 May 1958 looking aft over the quarterdeck shows the Faslane jetty in use by operational warships. The depot ship ADAMANT, HQ ship of the 3rd Submarine Squadron, with a mix of submarines and minesweepers alongside. (N. MacFarlane)

By 6 August 1958 demolition was well underway. As with her sistership ANSON, the 14-inch gun barrels were amongst the first items to be recovered. (N. MacFarlane)

Work to remove the superstructure had almost been completed by January 1959. Even in this lightened state, the lack of freeboard, which made these ships so wet forward in active service, is quite apparent. (N. MacFarlane)

Despite having been laid up in the Gareloch since 1950, this picture of ANSON, taken on 5 March 1958, shows her in remarkably good condition. She had arrived at Faslane 3 months earlier on 17 December 1957, though very little work appears to have been done. Closer inspection reveals that the masts have already been removed as has probably much of the upper superstructure. (N. MacFarlane)

Still looking almost every bit the battlehip, the first of the 14- inch barrels of ANSON's "A" turret had been severed by 4 March 1958.
(N. MacFarlane)

Despite the appearance of the previous pictures, this view of ANSON, from aft looking forward, shows the extent of the demolition work by 5 March 1958. Most of the after superstructure has gone, as have the funnels and masts. All four twin 5.25-inch turrets of the starboard battery have been removed.
(N. MacFarlane)

By 28 March the scrapyard workers had removed the upper deck and were working along 1 deck. Here the barbette for "B" turret rises above the deck, the turret having been removed. (N. MacFarlane)

Taken on the same day, the rotating mechanism for the quadruple after turret and the mountings for the four barrels can clearly be seen. (N. MacFarlane)

By June 1959 all that remains of the submarine VULPINE is the partially dismantled pressure hull. The opening for one of the four bow mounted torpedo tubes is visible. VULPINE was fitted with a dummy schnorkel in place of the second periscope during the war to provide RAF crews a live target for recognition purposes. Post war she served with the Royal Danish Navy for 11 years as the STOREN.
(N. MacFarlane)

The stripped out pressure hull was cut into sections and craned ashore for final demolition. Here VULPINE's after section is landed, complete with propellors, "A" brackets and severed shafts.

(N. MacFarlane)

In this view, probably taken in early 1960, the cut down hulk of NEWCASTLE is almost ready to be moved to the beaching grounds for final demolition. In the foreground is the LST 3 VAAGSO (ex LST 3019) which arrived at Faslane for demolition in December 1959.

(N. MacFarlane)

The remains of the River class frigate WAVENEY at Troon on 7 August 1958. Converted to a Headquarters Landing Ship during WWII, she was mostly disarmed and spent most of the post war period in Reserve at Harwich, in the Gareloch and at Lisahally, Londonderry. She arrived at Troon on 9 November 1957 to be broken up by West of Scotland Shipbreaking Industries Ltd. (T.W. Ferrers-Walker)

Introduced during the war to keep the national shipbuilding capacity fully extended, the small corvettes of the Castle class were rapidly outmoded in the post war era. CARISBROOKE CASTLE arrived at Metal Industries, Faslane on 14 June 1958 and by August was reduced to a bare hull, although she is still instantly recognisable as a former member of the Castle class. (N. MacFarlane)

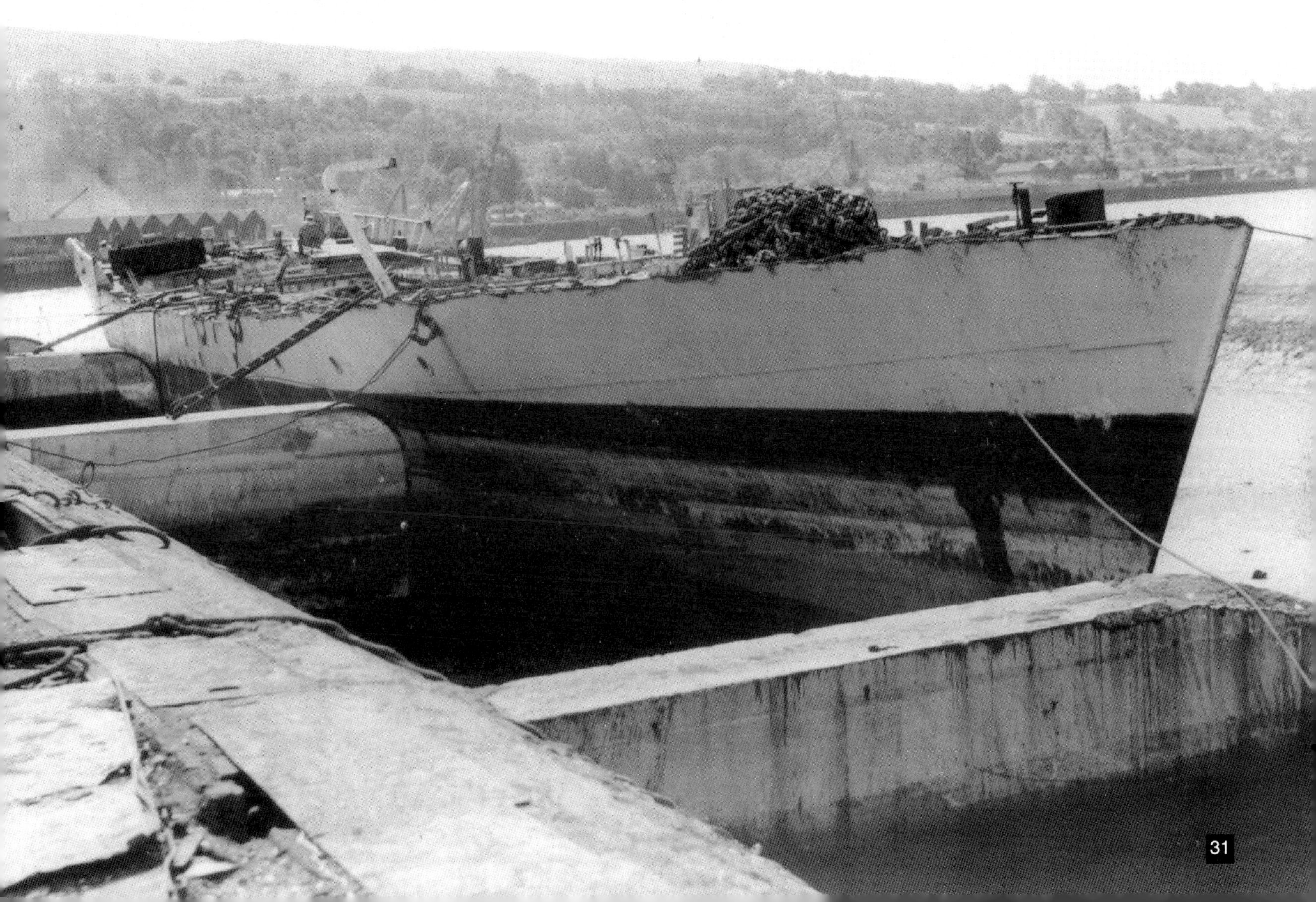

Modified on the stocks from the Loch class, the Bay class were completed as Anti-aircraft escort vessels. VERYAN BAY (ex- LOCH SWANNAY) was handed over to BISCO at Devonport and departed under tow of TRADESMAN on 19 June 1959. She is seen here at Charlestown shortly after arrival.
(N. MacFarlane)

Completed in March 1945 the Algerine class minesweeper LAERTES sailed for the East Indies in December of that year as part of the 10th Minesweeping Flotilla. On return to the UK in 1946 she was laid up at Harwich. In this 1959 shot she lies partially demolished at Barrow. Her sweep gear would appear to be still in situ on the quarterdeck. (J. Williams)

The difference in hull size between the early war Hunt class destroyer WHADDON (left) and the 1946 Bay Class frigate WIGTOWN BAY is quite apparent in this view of the two vessels at Faslane in June 1959. The amount of boot topping visible on the WIGTOWN BAY serves to indicate just how much effect a full fuel, ammunition and general store load has on the stability of these small vessels. (N. MacFarlane)

In refit at Simon's Town at the end of WWII, WILTON returned to Devonport on 10 Feb 1946 and reduced to Category B Reserve (a ship required for further service) until December 1949. A period of operations with the 4th Training Flotilla at Rosyth was followed by operations as an Air Target ship. WILTON was reduced to Class 2 Reserve (Stored, de-humified and manned with a nucleus crew, ready to sail for work up at 30 days notice) at Devonport (1952/53) before transferring to Cardiff and reducing to Extended Readiness (destored, de-equipped and laid up awaiting disposal) in 1955. She arrived at Faslane to be broken up on 4 December 1959 realising £22,900 in scrap.

(N. MacFarlane)

The unmodified T class submarines TUDOR (inboard) and TRENCHANT arrived at Faslane on 23 July 1963. Work on TUDOR is quite advanced, whilst TRENCHANT patiently awaits her turn. (N. MacFarlane)

With her upper casing removed the openings in the hull for two of TUDOR's forward torpedo tubes can be seen as can the two water-tight doors to the forward torpedo compartment. (N. MacFarlane)

TUDOR's conning tower is discarded ashore. These large sections were landed by crane for final stripping out and cutting down. (N. MacFarlane)

The former Light Fleet Carrier OCEAN at Faslane on 6 June 1962 . She had arrived a month earlier on 6 May, after 4 years in reserve at Devonport. Already the scrapping process has seen the removal of all superstructure and flightdeck flush with the gun sponsons.
(N. MacFarlane)

The Royal Navy's last battleship, VANGUARD, arrived at Faslane on 9 August 1960. In this view on 11 September the 15-inch gun barrels of "A" turret had already been removed, cut off at the face plate, as the cutters got to work on "B" turrets starboard gun. The secondary 5.25-inch turrets are still in place, though the close range platforms are empty, their weapons having been removed whilst the ship was laid up. (N. MacFarlane)

By 4 October 1960 the heavy breech ends had been removed from VANGUARD's now dismantled main turrets. (N. MacFarlane)

This cut through "A" turret shows to good effect the 11-inch side and 6-inch roof plates. Armour modifications to these WWI vintage turrets included replacing 9-inch armour on the front of the gun houses with 13-inch plate. The 4.5-inch roof armour was replaced by 6-inch non-cemented plate and the 2-inch armour under the gunhouse floor was increased to 3-inch. (N. MacFarlane)

Her gun barrels and breech ends laying severed on the jetty, VANGUARD rides ever higher in the water as more and more metal is recovered from the ship. (N. MacFarlane)

A cross section through the hull, taken in May 1961, just aft of the second starboard 5.25-inch mounting position shows off the thick cemented armour belt. This ranged in thickness from 13 inches abreast the machinery spaces to 14 inches abreast the magazines. This armour belt alone accounted for 4,666 tons of the ships displacement. (N. MacFarlane)

On 2 April 1962 what was left of VANGUARD was moved for the last time as the tug FLYING DUCK moved her from her berth at Faslane to the beaching grounds at Troon. (N. MacFarlane)

Two cut up sections of VANGUARD's stem await removal by rail. When built, VANGUARD cost £11,530,503, which included £3,186,868 for the armament. She was brought by BISCo for £560,000 and by the end of demolition had produced 38,800 tons of saleable material. (N. MacFarlane)

A 1964 picture of the incomplete LEVIATHAN in Fareham Creek. Work was suspended in May 1946 and she was towed to Portsmouth in July of that year, never to go to sea. She was used as a source of spare parts for the refit of KAREL DOORMAN (ex- VENERABLE) prior to her transfer to Argentina as the 25 de MAYO. She was eventually sold for scrap, arriving at Faslane on 27 May 1968 for breaking up. (Dr G. Watson)

After an active life in both war and peace the cruiser KENYA was sold for breaking up in 1962. She left Portsmouth under tow on 23 October 1962, arriving at Faslane 6 days later. Here the forecastle has become a dumping ground for metal awaiting craning ashore. The 6-inch turrets are now just a shell. (N. MacFarlane)

Although KENYA still appears to be pretty much intact, work continues around the after superstructure. Sections of the aftermast can be seen dumped on the quarterdeck. (N. MacFarlane)

Nearing the end of the lightening process, KENYA will soon be ready for towing to the beaching grounds. (N. MacFarlane)

By the mid 1960s Fareham Creek was awash with ships laid up in reserve or awaiting disposal (as this next series of pictures all taken on 27 August 1965) depicts. The Emergency War class destroyer CARRON was employed post war as a training ship. During a refit at Chatham in 1955 B gun was removed and a deckhouse put in its place. By 1957 all armament had been removed and the ship rejoined the Dartmouth Training Squadron, until July 1960. She then transferred to Portsmouth to assume the role of Navigation Training ship. She eventually paid off for disposal in March 1963 and arrived at Inverkeithing for demolition on 4 April 1967.

(M.J. Lennon)

The Early Battle class destroyer LAGOS awaits the call to the breakers yard. She was sold to P&W MacLellan in 1967 and arrived at Bo'ness in June of that year to be broken up. (M.J. Lennon)

The only clue to the fact that TRAFALGAR is laid up is the white tell tale mark at the waterline on the bows and the lack of an ensign. For a ship that has been in reserve since May 1963 she appears to be in remarkable condition. It was to be a further five years before she left for breaking up, arriving at Dalmuir on 8 June 1970. (M.J. Lennon)

Yet another Battle class laid up in Fareham Creek and ageing very well. SOLEBAY replaced VIGO as a Harbour Training Ship in April 1962. She left Portsmouth under tow on 7 August 1967 bound for scrapping at Troon. (M.J. Lennon)

The A class submarine AUROCHS was the only one of its class not to be modernised. A survey conducted in September 1964 found her to be in such poor condition that it was not considered worth refitting her. She lay at Gosport until 9 May 1966 when she was towed to Devonport for de-storing. She left Plymouth bound for Troon on 4 February 1967. She is seen here shortly afterwards with the conning tower and part of the casing removed. The trawler RONAY can also just be seen. (D.G. Thomas)

The Isles class trawler RONAY was completed in 1945 as a danlayer. Reduced to reserve at Devonport in February 1950 there followed a period of refit and preservation at Barry before a further period in reserve at Lisahally from 1955-65. She was sold to Loizos Aristophomous Loizides, Greece, on 29 June 1966. However, having defaulted on this deal the ship was then resold to West of Scotland Shipbreakers on 13 March 1967. Seen here at Troon in June 1967, her stern has already been removed and can be seen on the jetty. (D.G. Thomas)

The American S class submarine S29 rusting away at Pounds Yard in the 1960s. Launched in 1922, she was lent to the Royal Navy in 1942 and became P556. Following a battery explosion P556 was sold to Pounds in 1947. Despite an article in the Times in 1987 claiming that the scrap from the vessel was to be sold to Spain, it wasn't until August 1990 that the final sections of the vessel were lifted out of the water and cut up. (M.J. Lennon)

One of the numerically large Ton class, FLORISTON was completed on 19 August 1955 and saw service with the 108th MSS in the Mediterranean. She entered Operational reserve at Malta in 1958, but was towed to Gibraltar on 3 November 1959 to spend a further eight years in reserve both there and in the UK. On 27 May 1968 she was sold to Pounds Shipbreakers for conversion into a floating crane. Whether this happened or not is unknown as in this picture, taken a year later, she is seen leaving Portsmouth in tow of SUN XXII. Her funnel and all gear on the sweep deck has been removed, but there is little sign of any other conversion work. (M.J. Lennon)

Following seven years as Senior Officer Reserve Fleet's flagship and failed preservation attempts, SHEFFIELD left Portsmouth under tow for Rosyth Naval Base in 1967 so that she could be stripped of all usable spares. This even extended to removal of all nine 6-inch gun barrels - although as can be seen in this view the close range AA batteries remained! (N. MacFarlane)

SHEFFIELD is seen here at Faslane shortly after her arrival on 22 September 1967. The enclosed bridge and lattice masts were fitted during her final refit at Chatham in 1957. (N. MacFarlane)

A full house at Fountain Lake, Portsmouth, traditionally the home of the Reserve Fleet Ships. This picture was probably taken in 1964/65. From left to right are SHEFFIELD, the flagship of Senior Officer Reserve Fleet, RAME HEAD and an unidentified Ton class MCMV. On the middle jetty are CROSSBOW, RAPID and VOLAGE while on the extreme right is the destroyer CAVENDISH. In the foreground is the Inshore minehunter CHAILEY. Operational ships on the sea wall are from left to right PROTECTOR, CASSANDRA and DAINTY. Just visible in the background are a Tiger class cruiser in 3 Basin and behind the large crane to the right HARTLAND POINT.

(MoD/Crown Copyright)

The last of the famous WWII Illustrious class of aircraft carriers to see RN service, VICTORIOUS had undergone an extensive rebuild between 1950-58. However a cash strapped government looking for savings decided that the ship should be decommissioned following a small refit fire in 1967. She was decommissioned in November of that year and arrived at Faslane on 15 July 1969. This view taken from the centreline shows the $8^3/_4°$ angled flight deck fitted during the 1950's rebuild. (N. MacFarlane)

With the removal of the modernised flight deck the World War II ancestry of the VICTORIOUS becomes apparent. (N. MacFarlane)

HM Ships ADAMANT and DELIGHT laid up on the River Tamar after two very different careers. The Submarine depot ship ADAMANT was completed in 1942 and served in the Eastern Fleet until late 1944. There followed periods as Flag Officer, Reserve Fleet HQ Ship at Portsmouth, parent ship to the 3rd SM Squadron at Rothesay and 2nd SM Squadron at Devonport. She was listed for disposal in March 1966 and eventually arrived at Inverkeithing in September 1970 to be broken up. By comparison DELIGHT paid off for disposal in September 1967 after only 14 years in service. Her disarmed hulk arrived at Inverkeithing in December 1970 becoming the first of the Daring class to be scrapped. (S & J. Ninnes)

The former Ton class minesweeper HOUGHTON spent her service life in the Mediterranean and Far East with the 108th and 104th MSS. She returned to Devonport on 15 December 1970 to pay off. On 29 January 1971 she was sold to Vickers & Son (Eng) Ltd for commercial use at Plymouth and conversion to a tug. This venture obviously fell through as she is seen here before the end of the year in a partially dismantled state on a mudbank at Fleetwood. (I.W. Baxter)

Completed in 1940 BROWN RANGER was a member of the first class of tankers built after World War I specifically for the Admiralty. A veteran of the Mediterranean convoys and North Africa landings she was also present with the British Pacific Fleet for the reoccupation of Singapore and Hong Kong. Following a particularly active post war career she is seen here leaving Portsmouth in 1975 under tow of the tug INIGO LOPEZ TAPIR bound for breaking up in Spain. (M.J. Lennon)

Another former RFA bound for Spanish breakers. TIDESURGE was one of the first class of tankers to be designed specifically for fleet oiling duties. Completed in 1956 as TIDERANGE she was renamed in 1958. She left Portsmouth in 1977 under tow of the tug MUMBLES for breaking up in Spain. (M.J. Lennon)

Having spent her operational life overseas serving variously in the Mediterranean, Far East and Persian Gulf, PUNCHESTON returned to the UK to pay off in 1971. Sold to Pounds at Portsmouth in 1972, where she is seen here still wearing the badge of the 9th MSS. She was eventually broken up by Henderson Merez at Dartford in 1977. (M.J. Lennon)

Although launched in the closing years of World War II the cruiser LION and her two sisters were laid up incomplete on the Clyde in 1946 facing an uncertain future. Seven and a half years later in 1951 the decision was taken to complete the ships to a revised design. LION was moved to Swan Hunters at Wallsend for completion and was finally completed in February 1960. Just ten years later the cruiser made the short trip from Rosyth to T.W. Ward's shipbreaking yard at Inverkeithing on 24 February 1975.
(Dunfermline Central Library)

One of only a handful of World War II warships to survive into the 1980's ULSTER is manoeuvered towards Ward's Shipbreakers at Inverkeithing on 2 November 1980. Converted to a Type 15 Anti-submarine frigate at Chatham from 1954-57 she ended her days as a harbour training ship at Devonport. She was one of only three Type 15s to sport the raised bridge which was a feature of post war frigate design. (Dunfermline Central Library)

Paid off in 1978 further service for DEVONSHIRE was on the cards, however a proposed sale to Egypt fell through. She is seen here leaving Portsmouth on 20 May 1984 to be used as a target for the new Sea Eagle anti-ship missile and the Tigerfish torpedo. As a result of the torpedo attack DEVONSHIRE broke her back and sank on 17 July 1984, listing heavily to starboard before rearing up and sinking stern first. (M.J. Lennon)

On 8 December 1972 TENBY paid off into reserve at Devonport and was placed on the disposal list. A proposed sale to Pakistan in 1974 was cancelled and in June 1977 she was sold to T.W. Ward for breaking up at Briton Ferry. (Bill Whomes)

Not the most glamorous of purchases perhaps, but to a shipbreaker just a collection of metals to be recovered. The 1944 vintage Ocean Salvage Vessel, SALVICTOR, lies alongside at Briton Ferry whilst undergoing the recovery process. A varied career saw her attached to the British Pacific Fleet in 1945. There followed a survey of the ROYAL OAK in 1950, salvaging of Admiralty Floating Dock 9 at Singapore in 1952 and she was present at the Christmas Island Nuclear tests in 1957. In 1963 she was laid up in reserve at Pembroke Dock. She arrived at Briton Ferry in July 1970. (Bill Whomes)

HAMPSHIRE was the first of the County class GMD's to pay off - in April 1976. On 25 April 1979 she was towed from Chatham to be broken up at Briton Ferry where she is seen in the unusual setting of the Welsh countryside, nestled amongst rolling green hills and trees.
(Bill Whomes)

HM Ships FALMOUTH and LONDONDERRY (behind) laid up in Fareham Creek in November 1988. The two ships final role with the RN had been to provide training on steam machinery for Engineering Mechanicians and Engineering Ratings from HMS SULTAN. With the numbers of steam ships dwindling they became surplus to requirements. On 4 May 1989 FALMOUTH left Portsmouth under tow of the tug AFON GOCH for breaking in Spain whereas LONDONDERRY was sunk on 25 June 1989 as a target during a Joint Maritime Course. (A. Wright)

For the first eight years of her life SHIPHAM was placed in Operational Reserve at Rosneath (Scotland), stored ashore on a land cradle. Her Operational life was spent with the RNXS at Chatham. By 1986 she had been sold to Pounds shipbreakers at Portsmouth arriving there, reportedly, with a damaged stern. By the time this picture was taken in July 1989 it is apparent by the high water mark on the hull that she is no longer watertight. (R.M. Daniels)

The Leander class frigate NAIAD paid off at Portsmouth in May 1989 but, after only a short period in reserve, was selected to act as a floating test bed for trials of new construction techniques developed in the wake of the Falklands conflict. Renamed HULVUL the series of tests included fire, shock and blast trials. In March 1989 she was towed to ARE Dunfermline at Rosyth for phase two testing. She arrived back in Portsmouth on 5 August 1989. Trials continued, with HULVUL fitted with large box girders welded to the hull. She is seen here leaving Portsmouth for the final time on 24 September 1990 to be sunk as a target. The destructive nature of the trials is evidenced by the large sections of replaced steel plate and the bulge in the hull visible by the break in the forecastle. (M.J. Lennon)

As this book was published the question was could SCYLLA, the last of the Leander Class frigates still in the UK, become a tourist attraction for divers? Decommissioned on 14 December 1993 the ship has become the centre of attention for the Artificial Reef Consortium, who would like to sink her as an attraction off the Cornish coast. As the last Devonport built warship there is also interest from West country preservation groups. The only thing that is certain is that SCYLLA's future is anything but certain. (R. Lindfield)

Completed on 22 October 1954 HAVERSHAM was one of many inshore minesweepers to be placed into Operational Reserve at Gosport or Hythe. She was brought forward from reserve in 1963 and converted into a Torpedo Recovery Vessel (TRV), a role which she fulfilled until paying off in 1980. She is seen here on 11 September 1990 being broken up at Woolston, Southampton. Her wooden hull construction is evident as are the stern doors and ramps from her TRV conversion. (R. Lindfield)

Pounds Shipbreaking Yard at Portsmouth has been the final resting place for many submarines. By November 1995 OTTER is barely recognisable at this advanced stage of breaking. The remains of the two periscopes can be seen in the control room at the centre of the photograph.
(D. Hill)

OPPOSUM listing to starboard after the removal of her batteries in 1995. OTUS is secured on the outer trot with OTTER in between. Unlike most of the O Boats, which were fitted with GRP superstructure, OTTER was panelled in aluminium. This has been removed, exposing the bare ribs of her fin. (D. Hill)

OPPORTUNE in March 1996. The forward casing and pressure hull over the batteries have been removed exposing two sets of retractable mooring bollards and the forward torpedo loading hatch.
(D. Hill)

The breaking of ORPHEUS was well advanced when this picture was taken in June 1995. Her six 12 inch torpedo tubes can be seen protruding through the forward end of the pressure hull. (D.Hill)

TIPTOE photographed in September 1991. With the tide out work carries on removing the cast iron blocks from the keel. This view shows a cross section through the main ballast tanks in the area of the control room. (D. Hill)

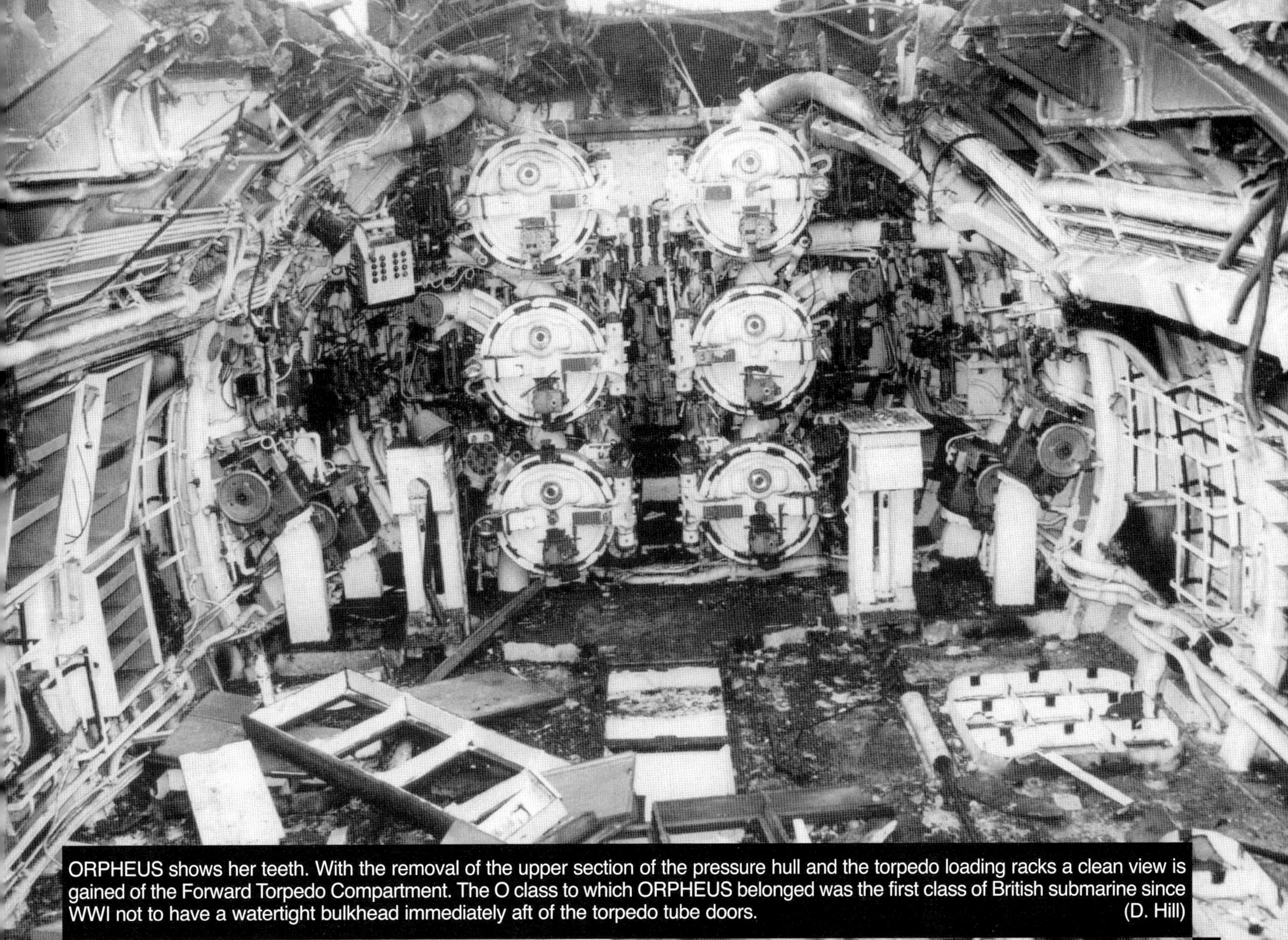

ORPHEUS shows her teeth. With the removal of the upper section of the pressure hull and the torpedo loading racks a clean view is gained of the Forward Torpedo Compartment. The O class to which ORPHEUS belonged was the first class of British submarine since WWI not to have a watertight bulkhead immediately aft of the torpedo tube doors. (D. Hill)

Pictured in July 1990 ARTEMIS was the last A class submarine to be scrapped. At this time the batteries and all aluminium superstructure had been removed. From this angle the broad beam of the double hull can be seen. Also the conning tower cylinder which contained the COs cabin.
(D. Hill)

OPPOSUM April 1996. Her two after torpedo tubes had been removed and the outlets blanked and welded. The starboard propellor has been removed but the rudder and hydroplanes can still be seen. The square tube is apparently a towing slip for mini subs. OPPOSUM was unusual in being fitted with a divers lockout chamber for covert operations. This was located in the forward casing. (D Hill)

OTUS and ORACLE seen together at Pound's Yard in Portsmouth in May 1997. The pressure tight chamber containing the electronics for the forward sonar equipment can be seen inside the bow superstructure. ORACLE had just been brought alongside on a high tide after being on her moorings in the harbour for over a year.
(D. Hill)

By 2002 there were 11 nuclear submarines laid up at Rosyth and Devonport whilst studies continue to investigate the best method of disposing of these vessels. In this picture five of them, CHURCHILL (without conning tower), DREADNOUGHT and SWIFTSURE, with the Polaris missile boats REVENGE and RESOLUTION (just visible on the extreme right) are stored afloat at Rosyth in February 2001. One of the four submarines stored at Devonport, COURAGEOUS, is to be put on public display as a visitor attraction at the dockyard from 2002. (D.Cullen)

The first of the Type 42 destroyers to be paid off, BIRMINGHAM, returns to Portsmouth on 19 May 2000 under tow of RT MAGIC having been stripped of all usable spares at Devonport. She left Portsmouth under tow of SANDSFOOT CASTLE on 20 October 2000 bound for Spanish breakers at Santander. Demolition was reportedly complete by July 2001. (Maritime Photographic)

Victims of the 1998 Strategic Defence Review sit in 3 Basin at Portsmouth providing an illustration of modern ships in reserve. To the right BRAVE is at Extended Readiness. All of her sensors are and weapons systems are covered and the ship has a reduced complement to maintain and regularly run up the systems. By comparison, her sistership LONDON has been paid off for disposal. Most of the reusable electronics and machinery has been removed and she is laid up dormant awaiting sale for further service or scrapping.
(Maritime Photographic)

With no sign of interest from a foreign navy BEAVER was sold for scrap and left Portsmouth on 21 February 2001 under tow of POSEIDON bound for Turkey. By 27 June of that year demolition was well under way at Alaiga, the hangar and flightdeck the only recognisable features. (Selim San)

Converted to a target ship in 1974 the former Type 15 frigate RAPID, moored at Milford Haven, bears the scars of several direct hits around the bridge area. She was docked at Devonport in 1977 for repairs after damage from missiles fired by BRISTOL.
(M.J. Lennon)

The end came for RAPID in 1981 in the Western Approaches after receiving two torpedo hits fired by the submarine ONYX. Her final moments are captured through the periscope of the attacking submarine. (MoD/Crown Copyright)

Making full use of a target is very important for a Sinkex. YARMOUTH was one of four targets to be deployed for a Joint Maritime Course in June 1987. Her fate included attack by 4 Sea Harriers from ARK ROYAL firing Sea Eagle missiles, having first identified her from the other targets. Lynx helicopters from MANCHESTER and BATTLEAXE then attacked with Sea Skua. An Exocet attack by BATTLEAXE was followed by Sea Dart and 4.5-inch gunfire from MANCHESTER. USS ANTRIM fired an SM-1 missile while two Danish frigates entered the fray with 76 mm gunfire. A bombing mission by Sea Harriers and Buccaneer aircraft carrying 1000lb Laser Guided Bombs and Martel missiles was also scheduled. In the event that the valiant YARMOUTH was still afloat MANCHESTER was planned to deliver the coup de grace with 4.5-inch gunfire! This picture was obviously taken early on in proceedings. It is not reported at which point during the onslaught she finally succumbed. (MoD/Crown Copyright)

INDEX